Published by
North Atlantic Books
Berkeley, California

Cover and interior art by Omileye Achikeobi-Lewis
Cover design by Jasmine Hromjak
Book design by Happenstance Type-O-Rama

Printed in Canada

My Heart Flies Open is sponsored and published by North Atlantic Books, an educational nonprofit based in Berkeley, California, that collaborates with partners to develop cross-cultural perspectives, nurture holistic views of art, science, the humanities, and healing, and seed personal and global transformation by publishing work on the relationship of body, spirit, and nature.

North Atlantic Books' publications are distributed to the US trade and internationally by Penguin Random House Publishers Services. For further information, visit our website at www.northatlanticbooks.com.

Library of Congress Cataloging-in-Publication Data

Names: Achikeobi-Lewis, Omileye, 1970– author.
Title: My heart flies open / Omileye Achikeobi-Lewis.
Description: Berkeley, California : North Atlantic Books, 2021. | Audience: Ages 4–8 | Audience: Grades 2–3 | Summary: "A sequence of 15 yoga poses and affirmations to help young readers process negative emotions, move through their feelings, and be at peace in their bodies"— Provided by publisher.
Identifiers: LCCN 2021004837 (print) | LCCN 2021004838 (ebook) | ISBN 9781623176136 (hardcover) | ISBN 9781623176143 (ebook)
Subjects: LCSH: Emotions—Juvenile literature. | Yoga—Juvenile literature. | Affirmations—Juvenile literature.
Classification: LCC BF511 .A24 2021 (print) | LCC BF511 (ebook) | DDC 152.4—dc23
LC record available at https://lccn.loc.gov/2021004837
LC ebook record available at https://lccn.loc.gov/2021004838

1 2 3 4 5 6 7 8 9 FRIESENS 26 25 24 23 22 21

My Heart Flies Open

Omileye Achikeobi-Lewis

North Atlantic Books
Berkeley, California

Breathing in and breathing out, I know

I AM *Love*.

I sit still with my legs crossed,
smile into my body, and rest in Easy Pose.

Feeling sad, invisible, and upside down,
I take a deep breath.

Breathing in and breathing out, I know

I AM *Stillness*.

Standing in the clouds,
I rest in Mountain Pose.

My breath and mind take me on a
fantastical trip. I bend this way and
that way with the wind.

Breathing in and breathing out,
I go with the flow and know

I AM *Life*.

I stand tall, inhale, and bend sideways
in Sideway Bending Mountain Pose.

I can surf the waves of all my emotions.

Breathing in and breathing out, I know

I AM *Bold*.

I stand with my feet and arms wide apart,
turn one foot to point to the side, then
bend my knee and gaze forward at all the
dreams waiting for me to catch them.
I rest in Warrior 2 Pose.

I feel tall like a tree standing still with every breeze, knowing life meets all my needs.

Breathing in and breathing out,

I AM *Grateful*.

I stand with my hands pointing toward the sunny sky. With one foot on my ankle or calf, I rest in Tree Pose.

Next time life challenges me, I can and
will say positive things to myself.

Breathing in and breathing out, I shout,

I AM *me*.

I stand with feet and hands apart like a
twinkling star. I turn one foot and point it to
the side. Keeping my arms straight, I bend my hips
and touch one hand to my calf or ankle. The other
hand points upward, love hearts in the air.
I rest in Triangle Pose.

Weeeee, whoosh, on my magic Alicorn,
I ride standing tall.

All my fears disappear into the
star-bright sky.

Breathing in and breathing out, I know

STILL I *Rise*.

I stand like a mountain, firm on my feet,
and kick one foot up behind me, catching it with the
same-side hand. I lift the other hand high into the
sky and now I am in modified Dancer Pose. I can go
a little further, and with a deep breath, I kick out
the foot resting in my hand until my leg stretches
out. With my other hand still high in the sky,
I rest in full Dancer Pose.

Emptied of doubts, I now feel great
on top of this mountain.

Breathing in and breathing out, I know

I AM *Enough*.

I stand with my feet and arms wide apart,
turn one foot to point to the side, then bend
my knee and gaze forward at all the dreams
waiting for me to catch them.
I rest in Warrior 2 Pose.

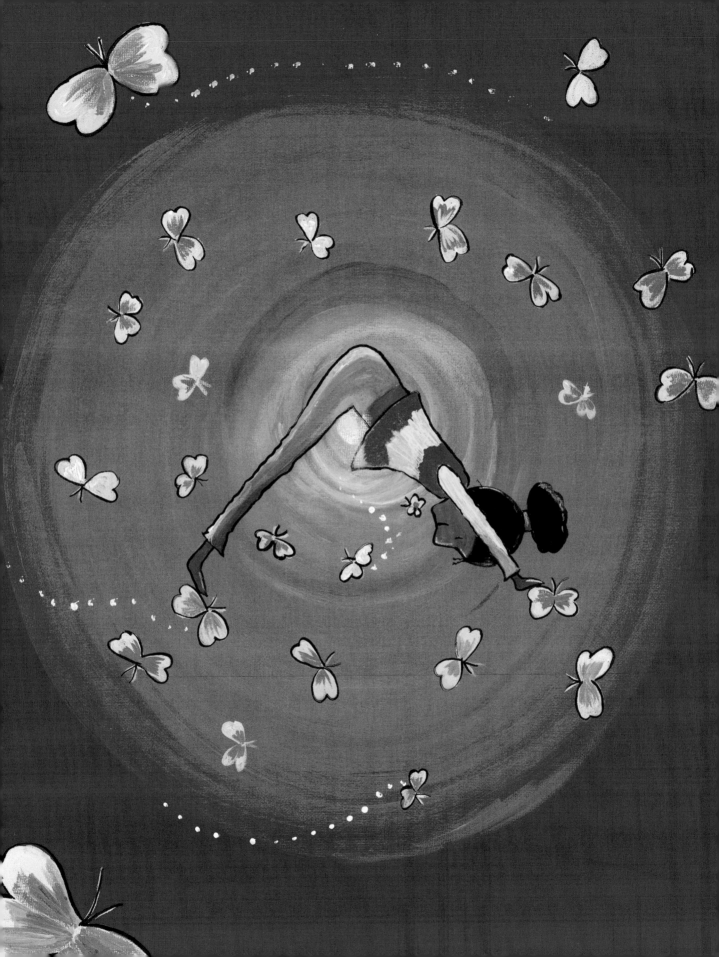

My breath transports me deeper into
my magical mind, where I discover a
starlit place that makes me feel alive.

Breathing in and breathing out, I know

I AM *Light*.

I rest on my hands and knees like a tabletop and
gently push up into Downward Dog Pose.

My heart flies open, releasing shimmering
butterflies of yummy feelings and smiles.

Breathing in and breathing out, I know

I AM *joy*.

I kneel on the earth and bend my body
slightly back until I can touch my feet.
I rest in Camel Pose.

I leap on top of the world and live among
the stars, planets, and all my dreams.
Now I feel at peace with me.

Breathing in and breathing out, I know

I .

I sit like a frog with my feet resting on
the floor. Then I leap with ease from
planet to planet in Squat Pose.

I love taking deep dives into my ocean
of dreams where I experience
oneness with everything.

Breathing in and breathing out, I know

I AM *Whole*.

I lie on my stomach and rest my hands gently on
the ground. Raising upward, I gaze into the
dolphin's eyes, resting in Upward Dog Pose.

Now I know the edge of my cliff does
not mean the end of the world, but is
the doorway to my marvelous life.

Breathing in and breathing out,

I AM ENDLESS *Possibilities*.

I look toward the warm pink sky.
Raising my chest and both legs upward,
I hold my ankles and rest in Bow Pose.

In every situation, I can blossom.

Breathing in and breathing out, I know

I AM *Peaceful*.

I cross my legs, with my back upright like
a lotus stalk, and relax in Lotus Pose.

I now know I can be soft but strong, and not get carried away with my hurly-burly emotions of anger, fear, sadness, and feeling down.

Breathing in and breathing out, I know

I AM *Fierce*

in a heart-based way.

I lie on the earth or an imaginary ocean, at last feeling complete. I am at total peace in Resting Pose.

ABOUT THE AUTHOR

Photo by Kai Lendzion

Omileye Achikeobi-Lewis is a mother, counselor, writer, artist, mindfulness teacher, kids' yoga teacher, and fifth-generation Vision Keeper. She hails from London and an African-Caribbean family and grew up with large Sunday dinners of rice and peas, curries, fried dumplings, and carrot juice. She remembers the constant chatter of world affairs and strange, magical, far-out cultural stories mixed in with spiritual life lessons. These Sunday dinners inspired her love of storytelling, cultures, peace, and art. Today, she loves helping kids and adults find the magic of the story within, the enchantment of cultures, the spellbinding power of the planet we live on, and the healing power of peace. Achikeobi-Lewis is also a diversity trainer and gives talks on mindfulness, Indigenous wisdom, and their power to create peace in our world, communities, and school systems.